It's My
STATE!

MARYLAND

The Old Line State

Derek Miller, Steven Otfinoski,
and Andy Steinitz

Cavendish
Square

New York

Published in 2019 by Cavendish Square Publishing, LLC
243 5th Avenue, Suite 136, New York, NY 10016

Library of Congress Cataloging-in-Publication Data

Names: Miller, Derek L., author. | Otfinoski, Steven, author. | Steinitz, Andy, author.
Title: Maryland / Derek Miller, Steven Otfinoski, and Andy Steinitz.
Description: New York : Cavendish Square, 2019. | Series: It's my state! (fourth edition) | Includes bibliographical references and index. | Audience: Grades 3-5.
Identifiers: LCCN 2017050416 (print) | LCCN 2017051080 (ebook) | ISBN 9781502626318 (library bound) | ISBN 9781502626158 (ebook) | ISBN 9781502644428 (pbk.)
Subjects: LCSH: Maryland--Juvenile literature.
Classification: LCC F181.3 (ebook) | LCC F181.3 .M55 2019 (print) | DDC 975.2--dc23
LC record available at https://lccn.loc.gov/2017050416

Editorial Director: David McNamara
Editor: Caitlyn Miller
Copy Editor: Nathan Heidelberger
Associate Art Director: Alan Sliwinski
Designer: Jessica Nevins
Production Coordinator: Karol Szymczuk
Photo Research: J8 Media

It's My STATE!

Table of Contents

SNAPSHOT
MARYLAND

The Old Line State

State Flag

The state flag, like the shield within the state seal, comes from the coat of arms of George Calvert, First Lord of Baltimore—a founding figure in Maryland history. The gold and black pattern that appears in two sections is from his father's family crest. The red and white crosses are taken from the coat of arms of his mother's family. The two images were combined to create the flag that was adopted by Maryland in 1904.

Statehood

April 28, 1788

Population

6,052,177
(2017 census estimate)

Capital

Annapolis

State Song

Maryland's state song is "Maryland, My Maryland." Its lyrics were written in 1861 by poet James Ryder Randall, and it was adopted as the state song in 1939. There have been efforts to replace it due to its pro-Confederacy lyrics.

HISTORICAL EVENTS TIMELINE

ca. 10,000 BCE

Native Americans coexist with ice age animals, such as mammoths.

1632

King Charles I grants Maryland to Cecilius Calvert, Baron of Baltimore.

1634

Cecilius's brother Leonard Calvert arrives in Maryland with two ships full of colonists. He founds Saint Mary's City.

State Seal

Unlike most state seals, Maryland's has two sides. The most commonly displayed side shows a farmer and fisherman standing on either side of a shield bearing Lord Baltimore's coat of arms. The words around the seal translate as "With favor wilt thou compass us as with a shield." The words in the banner are the state's unofficial motto and translate as "Strong deeds, gentle words." The less commonly shown side features Lord Baltimore as a knight on horseback.

State Tree

White Oak

The white oak is the state tree of Maryland. It is found throughout the state and most of the eastern United States. Growing up to 150 feet (46 meters) tall, the white oak is an impressive tree. Its name comes from its light-colored bark.

1729

The city of Baltimore is established.

1788

Maryland becomes the seventh state in the Union.

1814

Francis Scott Key writes "The Star-Spangled Banner" in Baltimore.

State Flower

Maryland's state flower is the black-eyed Susan. The flower has a black, circular center with golden petals radiating from it. As a result, its colors match the gold and black on the state flag. Black-eyed Susans are quite common in Maryland and are frequently planted beside roads and highways.

1947
Author Marguerite Henry writes *Misty of Chincoteague*, featuring the horses of Assateague Island.

1981
The National Aquarium opens in Baltimore.

1992
The Orioles Park at Camden Yards, a Major League Baseball ballpark, opens in Baltimore.

State Crustacean

Blue Crab

State Dog

Chesapeake Bay Retriever

State Reptile

Diamondback Terrapin

CURRENT EVENTS TIMELINE

2013

The Baltimore Ravens claim victory in Super Bowl XLVII.

2014

Maryland and neighboring states sign an agreement to protect the waters of the Chesapeake Bay.

2016

Maryland native Michael Phelps wins his twenty-third Olympic gold medal—more than any other Olympic athlete in history.

The Blue Ridge Mountains are just one of Maryland's scenic spots.

1 Geography

Maryland is a vibrant state of diverse people and businesses. Although it is quite small in size, it is home to over six million people as of 2017. The state is also diverse geographically. The east tends to be flat, while mountains rise in the west. Many different rivers and bays cut their way through the state. Maryland's defining feature is the Chesapeake Bay. Historically, it was extremely important to American development, linking early settlements to the Atlantic Ocean. Today, it is a celebrated symbol of the state. The Chesapeake Bay is a place where many families gather to spend time away from the bustle of modern life.

Maryland's Waterways

No matter where you are in Maryland, you are never very far from water. The Chesapeake Bay nearly cuts the state in half. The region between the bay and the Atlantic Ocean is called the Eastern Shore. The bay is the largest estuary in North America. An estuary is an area where

FAST FACT
Many people vacation in the beautiful Blue Ridge Mountains. Most famously, the mountains are home to Camp David—a vacation spot built for the president of the United States. Many presidents have used the camp to welcome important people visiting the country from around the world.

Chesapeake City is located near the northern end of Chesapeake Bay.

fresh river water and salty ocean water mix. Only 31 miles (50 kilometers) of the state face the Atlantic Ocean. The Chesapeake Bay, however, provides Maryland with a long and twisting shoreline that runs about 7,000 miles (11,250 km). The bay has many good harbors for boats.

The name Chesapeake comes from the Algonquian word "Chesepiooc." Some people say that was the name of a Native American village at the mouth of the bay. Others believe the word means "great shellfish bay." Either meaning fits the Chesapeake. For centuries, people have been catching oysters, crabs, and fish in its blue waters.

The Chesapeake provides a home and food for many different types of plants and animals. Fish of many types live in the bay and its marshes, wetlands, and tributaries.

The Great Falls of the Potomac are protected by the National Park Service.

More than four hundred rivers, flowing from six states, feed into the Chesapeake Bay. The largest are the Susquehanna River in the north and the Potomac River, which forms the state's southwestern border. Sixteen of Maryland's twenty-three counties border the Chesapeake. Annapolis, the state capital, is in Anne Arundel County on the bay's western shore.

There are no natural lakes in Maryland. All existing lakes have been made artificially by damming rivers. The largest of these, Deep Creek Lake, is 12 miles (19 km) long. It covers 3,900 acres (1,578 hectares), and it has 65 miles (105 km) of shoreline. Deep Creek Lake is a popular place to swim and fish for bass, pike, and trout.

Many Marylanders enjoy all the water that surrounds them. Some like to sail boats in the bay. Others prefer to water-ski. Sport fishing is popular in the Atlantic Ocean, and many people enjoy catching crabs in the bay and rivers.

In Cumberland, there are great views of the Alleghany Mountains.

Diverse Geography

Maryland's varied landscape is divided into three land regions. The eastern part—which is split by the Chesapeake Bay—is called the Atlantic Coastal Plain. This region includes the Eastern Shore—east of the bay—as well as part of the Western Shore. The area is dotted with marshes and swamps. Much of the fertile land is used for growing crops and raising chickens. The Atlantic Coastal Plain is home to Baltimore, Maryland's largest city. Ocean City, a popular beach town, is also located there. Only about seven thousand residents live in Ocean City year-round, but millions of tourists visit each summer.

Maryland borders Pennsylvania, Delaware, Virginia, West Virginia, and Washington, DC.

Maryland's Borders

Captain John Smith (1580–1631) was one of the first Englishmen to explore the Chesapeake Bay and surrounding land. He was impressed by the land, with its many rivers and waterways. At the time, rivers were used instead of roads for all sorts of transportation. People and goods traveled by ship rather than by land.

John Smith made detailed maps of the bay and the rivers running into it. Yet disagreements over boundaries soon cropped up in the New World. Lord Baltimore was granted a charter for Maryland in 1632. In 1681, William Penn received a royal charter for the new colony of Pennsylvania. However, the two charters assigned some of the same land to both provinces. Maryland felt that its charter gave them a wide swath of Pennsylvania—including its primary city, Philadelphia. Compromise on this issue seemed possible. But before it could be settled, the entirety of modern-day Delaware was also given to Pennsylvania. This was despite the fact that Delaware was clearly part of Maryland's charter. Neither side was willing to compromise on the huge border dispute.

The issue was so heated that violence broke out in Cresap's War during the 1730s. Eventually, the issue was settled by the surveyors Charles Mason and Jeremiah Dixon. They completed their survey of the Mason-Dixon Line in 1767, more than eighty years after the border dispute began. Their line decided the border of Maryland and Pennsylvania. It was drawn 15 miles (24 km) south of Philadelphia.

By this point, Delaware was a colony in its own right and was no longer a point of contention. The Mason-Dixon Line would resurface in American history when it was referenced as the border between slave states and Free States. At that time, Pennsylvania was a Free State. Maryland was a slave state.

A marker stands at the Mason-Dixon Line.

West of the Atlantic Coastal Plain stretches a wide area called the Piedmont. The plateau's hills and valleys contain most of the state's dairy farms. The Appalachian Region is located in the western "panhandle." Two mountain ranges—the Alleghenies and Blue Ridge—are part of the larger Appalachian range. The region's apple orchards thrive in the cooler weather. Its forests provide many jobs. The Appalachians were formed about 230 million years ago. They are the oldest mountains in North America. At Hancock, Maryland, in the Appalachian Region, the state is less than 2 miles (3.2 km) wide from north to south. That is the narrowest width recorded in any state.

The Blue Ridge Mountains extend as far south as northern Georgia and cut across a narrow strip of Maryland. They form one of the loveliest areas of the state. Their name comes from the blue haze that appears to hang over the mountains. The Allegheny Mountains lie in the westernmost part of Maryland. At 3,360 feet (1,024 m), Backbone Mountain in the Alleghenies is the highest peak in the state.

Climate

Eastern Maryland can be hot and humid in summer. Average temperatures approach 90 degrees Fahrenheit (32 degrees Celsius) in July and August. The area has mild winters, thanks to warm ocean breezes created by the Gulf Stream. The Gulf Stream is a warm ocean current that flows north from the Gulf of Mexico. The mountainous region in Western Maryland is considerably cooler and gets the most snowfall in the state. Up to 110 inches (279 centimeters) of snow can fall in certain parts of the state every year. The state receives an average of 41 inches (104 cm) of rain a year.

The flooding from Hurricane Isabel caused millions of dollars in damages.

Violent storms and hurricanes are rare in Maryland. An exception was Hurricane Agnes, which struck the Maryland coast in June 1972. In Maryland, the hurricane caused $110 million in damages and took nineteen lives. In September 2003, Hurricane Isabel caused the worst flooding along the Chesapeake coast in seventy years. In Baltimore, water levels rose 8 feet (2.4 m). The storm caused $410 million in damages statewide.

Wildlife

Maryland once had large wild animals such as cougars, elk, and bison. But people killed or drove away most of them. The only big mammal left in large numbers is the white-tailed deer. Black bears, once a rare sight in Maryland, are becoming more common in the western mountains. They have even been spotted on the Eastern Shore. But if you walk through wooded areas, you are more likely to come upon many smaller animals. These include raccoons, muskrats, gray squirrels, and red foxes.

The Chesapeake Bay's marshes are home to thousands of water birds. They include many kinds of ducks, terns, and geese. The great blue heron can be found along the state's many rivers and streams, where it catches fish. With its long, pointed bill and thin, stork-like legs, it is the largest American heron.

Maryland hunters stalk game birds, such as quail, mourning doves, ducks, and ring-necked pheasants. Hunters often use the state dog, the Chesapeake Bay retriever, to find the game birds they have shot. No one knows for sure how this dog breed developed in Maryland. One story goes that a British ship was wrecked off the coast in the early 1800s. Two Newfoundland dogs were saved from the ship and bred with local dogs. Over time, they produced a new breed.

Bay retrievers are highly intelligent and very loyal dogs. Sometimes they are trained to sniff out drugs for law enforcement officers or to perform rescue work. These dogs are so friendly that they are brought to hospitals and nursing homes to cheer up patients.

Chesapeake Bay retrievers are good companions for hunters.

Marylanders have not had as healthy of a relationship with their state bird, the Baltimore oriole. The oriole was given protection under state law in 1882 and was further protected under the state's Nongame and Endangered Species Conservation Act in 1975. Despite these laws, the bird's population has been declining. Much of its habitat has been destroyed by the construction of offices, stores, and factories. Also, many orioles have died from eating insects containing poisonous pesticides.

The Chesapeake Bay is full of many kinds of fish—such as shad, drumfish, and striped bass— that are fished commercially. In the ocean, sport fishers hook their lines to catch marlins, which resemble swordfish and can weigh more than 1,000 pounds (450 kilograms). In the rivers and streams, trout and perch are favorite catches.

Maryland's Biggest Cities

(Population numbers are from the US Census Bureau's 2017 projections for incorporated cities.)

Baltimore

Frederick

1. Baltimore: population 611,648

Nicknamed "Charm City," Baltimore is Maryland's largest city. It is also known as the "city of neighborhoods" because of its numerous districts, such as the Inner Harbor. Baltimore is known for its science and health industries.

2. Frederick: population 71,408

Frederick, in Central Maryland, is an eighteenth-century century town known for its shops, galleries, restaurants, and antique stores. Visitors and residents also enjoy the National Museum of Civil War Medicine, Monocacy National Battlefield, the Weinberg Center for the Arts, and more.

3. Gaithersburg: 68,710

Gaithersburg has two main areas. Olde Town is a historic district on the east side of town, which includes businesses and landmarks. The west side of town has more modern businesses, shopping, and wealthy neighborhoods.

4. Rockville: population 68,401

Located northwest of Washington, DC, Rockville is part of the Baltimore-Washington metropolitan area. The Rockville area is home to many software and biotechnology companies. The city offers theater, shopping, and dining.

5. Bowie: population 58,859

Bowie (BOO-eee), located between Baltimore and Washington, DC, boasts walking trails and more than fourteen parks. Attractions include the Belair Mansion, the National Capital Radio and Television Museum, and the Bowie Railroad Museum.

6. Hagerstown: population 40,306

Hagerstown, in West-Central Maryland, has a lot of cultural attractions, such as the Maryland Theatre, Maryland Symphony Orchestra, and the Washington County Museum of Fine Arts. Hagerstown is home to the Western Maryland Blues Fest.

7. Annapolis: population 39,321

On the bank of the Chesapeake Bay is Annapolis, the capital of Maryland. Annapolis is a very historically important city. It was the first peacetime capital of the United States, from 1783 to 1784. Congress ratified the Treaty of Paris in Annapolis, which ended the American Revolution.

8. Salisbury: population 32,807

Nicknamed "the crossroads of Delmarva," Salisbury is the commercial center of the **Delmarva Peninsula**, part of which Maryland occupies, along with Delaware and Virginia. It is the largest city on the Eastern Shore, and it is popular for its proximity to the Chesapeake Bay and the Atlantic Ocean.

Gaithersburg

9. College Park: population 32,303

Home to the flagship campus of the University of Maryland, this city is just minutes from Washington, DC. Half of the city's residents are students, but many people who work in Washington live in this bustling suburb.

10. Laurel: population 25,906

Laurel is a small city that is home to many people who work in nearby Washington, DC, and Baltimore. Laurel has small theaters, parks, and year-round festivals, including a street fair along the city's main street.

Annapolis

Maryland's Five Biggest Unincorporated Cities

Some of Maryland's biggest cities are **unincorporated**, meaning they have no city government. Here's a look at the top-five unincorporated cities in Maryland by population.

1. Columbia: population 103,439

Located between Baltimore and Washington, DC, Columbia is the second-largest city in Maryland overall. It was founded in 1967 as a planned community meant to improve the lives of its residents. Today, it is frequently ranked as one of the country's best small cities to live in. *Money* magazine ranked it as number one in 2016.

Columbia

2. Germantown: population 90,494

Germantown is a city near Washington, DC. It is governed as part of Montgomery County. The city got its name from its European immigrants, and today it remains a very diverse city.

3. Silver Spring: population 78,038

Silver Spring borders the northern edge of Washington, DC. It is home to numerous companies and even the National Oceanic and Atmospheric Administration of the federal government.

Silver Spring

4. Waldorf: population 72,413

Waldorf is just to the south of Washington, DC. It is a bedroom community—most people who live there commute to work outside of Waldorf. Residents frequently work in either Washington, DC, or the nearby Andrews Air Force Base.

5. Glen Burnie: population 69,060

Glen Burnie is the seventh most populous city in Maryland overall. It is located at the northern end of Anne Arundel County. It is considered a suburb of Baltimore, but it is also a short commute away from Annapolis—Maryland's capital.

The oldest rockfish ever caught in Maryland was thirty-one years old.

Marshes are home to the diamondback terrapin, Maryland's state reptile. Before laws were passed to protect them, diamondbacks were nearly hunted into extinction for their meat.

The Wild Horses of Assateague Island

Perhaps Maryland's most interesting animals are the wild horses of Assateague Island. This long, narrow island sits off Maryland's Atlantic coast. Two million visitors come to Assateague Island National Seashore each year to see the horses.

How the horses got there is a mystery. One legend claims that a Spanish ship ran aground on the island many years ago, and the horses on board escaped. But many people now believe the horses are the descendants of workhorses that farmers brought to the island and let graze

Assateague Island's wild horses are a big draw for tourists.

FAST FACT

The rockfish is Maryland's state fish. The same species of fish is called the striped bass or striper. Catching rockfish is popular among Marylanders. There is even a sports fishing industry built around the fish. Some people make their living taking tourists out to catch tasty rockfish, which can also make impressive trophies.

What Lives in Maryland?

Flora

Black Tupelo Black tupelo trees are also called black gum, or simply gum trees. A black tupelo can grow to heights of 120 feet (36 m). They are commonly planted as ornamental (decorative) trees due to their beautiful autumn foliage. Black tupelo trees are an important part of the local ecosystem, providing food for bees.

Christmas Fern Christmas ferns are common across the state in the wild and in gardens. The fern's name comes from the fact that it remains green throughout the winter—including the Christmas season. The Christmas fern is quite small, rarely growing taller than 3 feet (1 m).

Flowering dogwood

Flowering Dogwood This small tree is native to the state. The flowering dogwood gets its name from its flowers that appear in the spring. Depending on the tree, flowering dogwoods' blooms can range from brilliant white to bright pink or red. The tree features red foliage in the fall and red berries in the winter. These characteristics make flowering dogwoods a staple in many yards and gardens in Maryland.

Northern Highbush Blueberry This blueberry bush grows wild in Maryland. It was cultivated by Native Americans before the first Europeans arrived and continues to be a popular plant to grow. Its berries are also an important source of food for wildlife.

Sassafras This tree is found across Maryland. It has a long history of human use. Native Americans used its bark and roots to make many different medicines. Today, it is most famously used to make root beer. However, it is also used to make various products like soap, oil, and tea.

Fauna

Delmarva Fox Squirrel The Delmarva fox squirrel was endangered until 2015. It only lives in small parts of Maryland's Eastern Shore and Delaware. Its most notable characteristic is its large size. Delmarva fox squirrels are twice as big as the much more common gray squirrels that live in the region.

Great blue heron

Great Blue Heron These birds are a common sight in Maryland. They live in the state's many wetlands and along the shore. The great blue heron can grow quite big. Its majestic blue wings can stretch up to 6.6 feet (2 m).

Baltimore Oriole The Baltimore oriole is the state bird of Maryland. Its name comes from the fact that it is black and orange—the same colors that appear on Lord Baltimore's coat of arms and now on the Maryland flag. As a result of the bird's status and beautiful appearance, Baltimore's Major League Baseball team is named after it.

Baltimore oriole

Osprey These birds of prey are found throughout most of Maryland. They build their nests near bodies of water, using broken branches and other material. Osprey nests can be seen on many manmade structures in the bay and surrounding rivers. Ospreys prey on fish and often share the same habitat as bald eagles in Maryland.

Shortnose Sturgeon The shortnose sturgeon is one of the many fish that reside in Maryland. They used to be quite common, but now they are listed as an endangered species due to fishing, pollution, and the damming of rivers. Shortnose sturgeons have a very distinctive appearance, with bony plates running along their spine.

Shortnose sturgeon

on the marsh grasses. The grasses are not very nutritious, so the horses of Assateague grow only to the size of ponies.

The wild horses still survive on the marsh grasses today. This has become a problem. The marsh grass holds the sand together to form dunes. If new dunes are not created, the ocean waters will eat away at the land. One day the island will be covered by water.

Scientists have developed ways to control the wild horse population. State workers shoot darts at the female horses, called mares. The darts' contents prevent the mares from having babies. Each year, some of the horses are also rounded up and sold at auctions. These measures keep the number of horses down and help protect the island.

Save the Bay

One challenge confronting Maryland is how to protect the Chesapeake Bay from pollution. Across the state, you can see bumper stickers on cars that read "Save the Bay." The issue is close to many people's hearts since the bay is a common vacation spot. Some Marylanders also depend on the bay for their livelihood.

Maryland has strict laws to prevent pollution from entering the bay. However, fertilizer used in states that do not even border the bay enters rivers that then empty into the Chesapeake. This is known as runoff—a kind of pollution that comes from both farms and lawns.

In 2014, a landmark agreement was signed by Maryland and neighboring states to protect the bay. The Chesapeake Bay Watershed Agreement hopes to prevent further pollution of the bay and repair past damage.

Ocean City is one of Maryland's most famous tourist attractions. The Eastern Shore resort town lies on the sandy beach of the Atlantic Ocean. People from all over the state and country go there to bask in the sun and walk the length of its famous boardwalk.

The 3-mile (5 km) boardwalk is lined with hundreds of stores, restaurants, and hotels. There are even two amusement parks with Ferris wheels, roller coasters, and water slides overlooking the ocean. Many Maryland favorites are on the boardwalk, like Thrasher's French Fries and Shriver's Salt Water Taffy—dating to 1929 and 1898, respectively.

Ocean City also serves as a launching point for all kinds of adventures. You can rent a kayak, jet ski, or surfboard to spend some time on the water. Chartered fishing vessels take passengers out to see what they can catch. If you want to stay on land, there are plenty of options too. There are more than a dozen golf courses in the area, as well as a 100-mile (161 km) bike trail.

Beyond Maryland's oceanfront attractions, there are also many historical sites and museums to see. The Harriet Tubman **Underground Railroad** National Historic Park is across the scenic Eastern Shore in Church Creek. Visitors can learn about Tubman's important work in the area where she helped save many African Americans from slavery. It is a legacy of bravery that all Marylanders can be proud of.

Ocean City Boardwalk and Other Top Attractions

The Harriet Tubman Underground Railroad National Historic Park is a monument to one of Maryland's most important people.

Ocean City's boardwalk has something for everyone.

Maryland's first residents lived in wigwams similar to these.

2 The History of Maryland

Maryland has a rich past. It was colonized at an early date and played a leading role in early American history. The state was also an important battleground during the War of 1812—and is the site where the words to "The Star-Spangled Banner" were composed. Before the arrival of the Europeans, it was home to many Native American tribes, each with their own rich culture.

Native Americans in Maryland

Native Americans first came to Maryland around 10,000 BCE. The only hints to their cultures are artifacts such as pottery, arrowheads, and burial sites.

By the 1600s, various Algonquian-speaking tribes were living along the Chesapeake Bay. The Piscataway and Patuxent peoples lived west of the bay. The Choptank, Nanticoke, and Assateague lived on the Eastern Shore. The

FAST FACT
Maryland's first European settlers were carried aboard two ships, the *Ark* and the *Dove*. Soon after setting sail from England, the ships encountered a storm. The *Dove* disappeared. Those aboard the *Ark* assumed the *Dove* had sunk and continued on their way. Six weeks later, after both ships crossed the Atlantic, the ships rejoined each other in the Caribbean before setting off for Maryland.

Iroquoian-speaking Susquehannock settled in the north at the head of the bay.

Some lived in long huts. Others preferred oval wigwams made from wood and covered with bark or matting. Villages were small and consisted of only several hundred people. The men hunted, fished, and gathered shellfish from the bay. The women grew corn, squash, beans, and tobacco. Many tribes moved inland for the winter. However, European newcomers would soon challenge this way of life.

John Smith was the first European to visit Maryland.

Europeans Arrive

Italian explorer Giovanni da Verrazzano may have been the first European to see Maryland. He sailed past the Chesapeake Bay in 1524 while exploring the shoreline of America for the king of France. The first explorer to actually visit the area was Englishman John Smith. In 1608, Smith sailed up the Chesapeake Bay. He described the area that would become Maryland as a "fruitful and delightsome land!"

However, Smith decided to return to the Jamestown colony in Virginia. In 1607, he had helped found that colony. Jamestown was the first permanent English settlement in America. William Claiborne, another member of the Virginia colony, also began exploring to the north. He was attracted to the Chesapeake Bay and saw its potential for colonization. Claiborne set up a trading post on Kent Island in the bay in 1631. That was the first permanent European settlement in present-day Maryland.

At the same time, George Calvert, the first Lord Baltimore, was seeking a land grant in the region from King Charles I of England. At the time, many European Protestants and Catholics

George Calvert is either called the first Lord Baltimore or the first Baron Baltimore.

did not get along. In England, where the rulers were Protestant, laws punished people who practiced Catholicism. England's American colonies had similar laws. Calvert wanted Maryland to be a safe place for Catholics to settle. Calvert died in 1632, before his colony could be officially chartered. A few months later, his son Cecilius Calvert received the land grant instead. He named the colony Maryland after Charles I's wife, Queen Henrietta Maria. (The English often called her Queen Mary.) In March 1634, Cecilius's brother Leonard landed in Maryland with two ships carrying settlers. He founded the settlement of Saint Mary's City in Southern Maryland. The city became the first capital of the colony.

In 1649, the legislature passed the Act Concerning Religion. The law gave all Christians living in Maryland the right to choose how they worshipped. Passed to protect the Catholic minority, it is one of the first laws granting religious freedom in America.

A British Colony

The Calvert family ruled the Maryland colony despite several disputes, including a feud with Claiborne over Kent Island. In 1689, colonists seized the government and demanded that the king take over the colony. The first royal governor arrived in 1692. Two years later, the capital was moved from Saint Mary's City to Anne Arundel Town. Later, Anne Arundel Town's name would be changed to Annapolis.

Maryland farmers started tobacco plantations along the rivers that empty into the Chesapeake Bay. They needed many workers for these big farms. In 1664, slavery—the enslavement of Africans for life—became legal in the colony.

FAST FACT
Native Americans have left a lasting legacy in Maryland. Many places are still called by the names that Native Americans gave to them. For example, the word "Chesapeake" is thought to be a Native American word meaning "great shellfish bay." Many river names, like Nanticoke and Choptank, also have Native American roots.

Maryland Day

On March 25, 1634, about 140 English settlers landed on Maryland's shores. It was the first attempt to found a major settlement in the province of Maryland. The settlers disembarked from two ships, the *Ark* and *Dove*, at Saint Clements Island in the Potomac River. They built defenses there and entered negotiations with the local Native Americans, the Piscataway. The Piscataway agreed that the English could build a settlement that would become Saint Mary's City.

March 25 is now Maryland Day to commemorate the first landing of the settlers in Maryland. The holiday was first adopted by the state board of education as a day for students to learn about Maryland history. In 1916, Maryland Day became an official state holiday when the state government adopted it. It is always celebrated on March 25 unless that date falls on a Sunday. In that case, the holiday is celebrated the following Monday.

Schools and businesses in Maryland do not close on March 25. Instead, it is a day to celebrate Maryland history. Schools, from kindergartens to universities, often hold events to educate students about state history. Many local businesses celebrate the day as well, with specials and patriotic events. Museums and historic sites across the state also commemorate Maryland Day. They frequently open their doors free of charge.

In this illustration, Leonard Calvert plants a cross, marking Maryland's first settlement.

Prior to then, some blacks had been brought to the colony to work, primarily from the Caribbean. Even after slavery became law, however, both black and white indentured servants were more common than slaves until the 1700s. Indentured servants were people whose passage to America was paid in exchange for work for a master, usually for up to seven years. After that period, the servant was freed. Mathias de Sousa was a black indentured servant who arrived with the first colonists in 1634. He soon gained his freedom. In 1642, he became the first black man to serve in the state's general assembly.

The Thomas Stone National Historic Site is an example of a Maryland plantation.

By the 1700s, African slaves had replaced most white indentured servants on the large tobacco plantations. Slaves led miserable lives. They were forced to work long hours six days a week, and they were housed in shabby cabins.

The colony continued to grow. During the 1700s, European settlers forced many Native Americans to move west, out of Maryland. Some Native Americans were killed when they refused to give up their land. Others died of diseases brought by the settlers from Europe.

The Revolutionary War

A larger conflict was growing between Great Britain and its American colonies. While tobacco farmers and some other Marylanders were on good terms with the British, many colonists wanted independence. In 1774, Maryland patriots in Annapolis copied the Boston Tea Party of 1773. They protested the British tax on tea by burning a British ship, the *Peggy Stewart*, and its cargo of tea.

War broke out in April 1775. Not much fighting took place in Maryland during the

This painting from the early 1900s shows the burning of the *Peggy Stewart*.

The Battle of Long Island led to Maryland's nickname: the Old Line State.

American Revolution. Maryland soldiers, however, fought bravely in many battles.

The colonists won their independence in 1783. The thirteen colonies—now states—struggled to find a new form of government. In September 1786, Annapolis hosted a states' convention. Delegates discussed the issues of trade and business. They agreed to meet again in Philadelphia in 1787.

At the Philadelphia convention, delegates wrote the US Constitution. It was a bold plan for a national government. On April 28, 1788, Maryland became the seventh state to ratify, or approve, the Constitution.

The War of 1812

In 1812, the United States once again went to war with Great Britain. People sometimes call the War of 1812 the second American Revolution. This time, a good deal of fighting took place in Maryland. In 1813, the British entered the Chesapeake Bay. There, the British attacked ships and raided towns. In September 1814, one month after British forces burned much of Washington, DC, they attacked Baltimore. American lawyer Francis Scott Key was aboard a truce boat, awaiting the release of an American doctor imprisoned by the British. From the boat, he watched the British **bombard** Fort McHenry, which guards the entrance to Baltimore harbor. All day and into the night on September 13, Key watched British ships fire rockets and exploding bombs at the fort.

To Key's joy, the next morning the American flag still flew over the fort "by the dawn's early light." The British retreated. Key began to write a poem about the event, and he finished it that

FAST FACT

During the American Revolution, some groups of soldiers were called a "line." At the Battle of Long Island, the Maryland line fought bravely. They held off the British so that George Washington could escape with most of his army. In doing so, they lost many brave men. According to tradition, it is Washington himself who named Maryland "The Old Line State" in their honor.

same night. Less than a week later, his poem, "Defense of Fort M'Henry," was published in a Baltimore newspaper. It was later set to the tune of an English song. It became "The Star-Spangled Banner." In 1931, eighty-eight years after Key's death, his patriotic song officially became the US national anthem.

The United States and Great Britain signed a peace treaty ending the War of 1812 in December 1814. (Because news traveled slowly at that time, a major American victory in the war, at the Battle of New Orleans, actually took place in January 1815.)

Francis Scott Key wrote a poem that would later become the national anthem.

The Civil War

Maryland made great strides in the 1800s in industry and development. The first national highway, called the National Road, was finished in 1818. It joined Cumberland, Maryland, with Wheeling, Virginia (now in West Virginia). Peter Cooper built one of the first American steam locomotives, *Tom Thumb*. The locomotive made its first run on the new Baltimore and Ohio Railroad in 1830. In 1844, Samuel Morse sent the first message over a telegraph line from Washington, DC, to Baltimore.

Today, Fort McHenry is a national monument.

The Baltimore and Ohio Railroad (shown here in 1858) was one of many innovations of the 1800s.

Native American Life

Maryland is a small but geographically diverse state. The Native American tribes that lived in the region at the time of the European settlement were distributed along those geographic lines. When the *Ark* and the *Dove* landed at what is now Saint Mary's City in Southern Maryland, they encountered members of the Piscataway. The Nanticoke and the Piscataway dominated the Eastern Shore. The Lenape lived in the northeast corner that today borders Pennsylvania and Delaware. The Susquehannock populated the hilly region north of present-day Baltimore, and the Tutelo and Saponi were found in the parts of the Piedmont that now include Montgomery, Howard, and Frederick Counties. The Ohio Valley tribes, including the Shawnee, lived in mountainous Western Maryland.

Saint Mary's City in the 1600s

Native Americans throughout Maryland had different customs. But in many ways, their daily lives had striking similarities. Most Native Americans in the area lived in longhouses or wigwams. They hunted and fished, and they grew crops such as corn, beans, and squash. They made their clothing from animal skins and grasses.

Much like in many other parts of the United States, the European settlers brought several epidemic diseases, including smallpox, measles, and **tuberculosis**, to Maryland with them. Native Americans lacked immunity to these new diseases. As a result, many Native Americans died.

The colonial expansion of Maryland drove out most of the rest of the Native Americans during the 1700s. Many were forced to move to reservations in Oklahoma and Kansas. These tribes still exist, but for the most part they did not return to Maryland.

Today, there are more than thirty thousand Native Americans in the state. However, there are no federally recognized tribes in Maryland. On January 9, 2012, Governor Martin O'Malley signed two executive orders making the Piscataway Indian Nation and the Piscataway Conoy Tribe the first tribes ever recognized by the state.

Many of Maryland's Native Americans lived in structures similar to these.

Spotlight on the Piscataway

The Piscataway tribe, also called the Conoy, is an Algonquian-speaking tribe that lived, and continues to live, along the Chesapeake Bay in Maryland. "Piscataway" means "where the waters blend." The Piscataway were one of the largest tribes in Maryland; however, after Europeans colonized the area, the population decreased.

Homes: Like many other Algonquian tribes, the Piscataway lived in longhouses. Longhouses were long and rectangular, and were of various lengths. The roofs were often barrel-shaped, and they were covered with bark or woven mats.

Trade: Trade was a very important aspect of Piscataway culture. The tribe often traded tools, food, and weapons with other Native American tribes. After the Europeans arrived in the seventeenth century, the tribe traded what they had with the Europeans for metal and firearms.

Art: The Piscataway people were talented potters. Their pottery had a practical purpose. They used pottery to store food and to protect their seeds before planting.

Dance: The Rabbit Dance was a dance that took place at Piscataway social dances. The Rabbit Dance called for the women to choose a male dance partner. According to legend, if a man refused, he would turn into a rabbit! The Ring Dance, or Hoop Dance, featured a dancer who picked up one hoop at a time. Each hoop helps to form a new symbol of nature, such as a turtle, eagle, or the world.

The Baltimore Riot of 1861 took place at the beginning of the Civil War.

All these achievements helped bring Americans closer together, but the issue of slavery moved them farther apart. By the mid-1800s, most people in the North opposed slavery. In the South, most people supported it. Harriet Tubman, a runaway slave from Maryland, helped many other slaves escape from the South. She was the most famous "conductor" on the Underground Railroad.

By early 1861, a number of Southern states had seceded, or broken away, from the United States (the Union). They formed the Confederate States of America. The people of Maryland were torn. Many wanted Maryland to remain in the Union, and it did. Yet some still relied on slave labor. Therefore, many people sided with the Confederacy. On April 19, a week after war began with Confederate forces attacking Fort Sumter in South Carolina, a riot broke out in Baltimore. A pro-Confederate mob attacked troops from Massachusetts who were traveling to Washington, DC. Four soldiers and twelve other people died in the riot. They were the first people killed in the Civil War.

More than seventy thousand Maryland soldiers fought in the war. About fifty thousand of them fought for the Union. Several important battles were fought in the state. The biggest was the Battle of Antietam on September 17, 1862.

General Robert E. Lee had invaded Maryland with 37,400 Confederate troops two weeks earlier. Under General George McClellan, fifty-six thousand Union soldiers met them at Antietam Creek near Sharpsburg. The fighting began in the early morning and continued throughout the day. When the battle ended—with a Union victory—more than twenty-three thousand soldiers on both sides were wounded or dead. It was the bloodiest one-day battle of the Civil War.

The Battle of Antietam was one of the most deadly battles of the Civil War.

After Antietam, Lee retreated to Virginia. The Union victory gave President Abraham Lincoln the opportunity to issue an early version of his Emancipation Proclamation. In the final proclamation, effective January 1, 1863, Lincoln declared that all slaves in Confederate-controlled territory "shall be then, thenceforward, and forever free." The emancipation did not apply to slaves in Maryland, though. This is because Maryland was part of the Union.

In 1864, Maryland adopted a new state constitution that abolished slavery. It also denied Confederate supporters the right to vote. The war ended in Union victory the following year. In December 1865, the Thirteenth Amendment to the US Constitution officially ended slavery throughout the United States.

Two World Wars—and a Depression

Soldiers train at Camp Admiral (now known as Fort Meade) during World War I.

In the years following the Civil War, Maryland became a leader in science and education. Johns Hopkins University was founded in Baltimore in 1876. The world-famous Johns Hopkins Hospital opened thirteen years later. Today, the hospital and school remain important research centers. Johns Hopkins doctors have discovered new treatments for tuberculosis and other diseases. In 1886, Baltimore opened one of the first free public library systems in the country.

The United States entered World War I in 1917. More than sixty-two thousand Marylanders served in the armed forces. The US Army established Aberdeen Proving Ground near the Chesapeake Bay in 1917 to test new weapons. Today, it is the oldest active proving ground. In Anne Arundel County, the War Department established a base that became known as Fort Meade. During the war, more than four hundred thousand soldiers passed through Fort Meade. It remains a major army base today.

During the 1930s, the Great Depression caused great hardship for Marylanders and people across the country. Thousands of banks failed, businesses closed, and millions of people were out of work. The US government created many new programs to help the nation recover. In Maryland, the government built a new town, called Greenbelt, not far from Washington, DC.

Marylanders have always treasured their waterways. Numerous lighthouses were built across the state to guide sailors into port and help them avoid running aground. The Cove Point Lighthouse is one of the state's most famous lighthouses. It sits on the western edge of the Chesapeake on a piece of land that extends into the bay. Its light warns ships to steer clear. Follow the instructions below to make a model of the Cove Point Lighthouse.

Building a Lighthouse

Materials

- 1 large Styrofoam cup
- Black construction paper
- 1 small, clear plastic cup
- 1 LED tealight candle
- Black marker
- Scissors
- Tape

Directions

1. Place the Styrofoam cup on a piece of black construction paper and trace around the base with the marker.
2. Cut out the circle you traced.
3. Flip the Styrofoam cup over. This is the base of your lighthouse. Draw a door and windows onto the Styrofoam.
4. Place the tealight candle on top of the upside-down Styrofoam cup.
5. Place the clear plastic cup upside-down on top of the candle to cover it.
6. Take the black circle of paper and make one cut to the center of the circle.
7. Slide the paper to the left of the cut over the right side to create a cone.
8. Tape the paper so it stays cone-shaped.
9. Tape your cone to the top of the lighthouse—this is the roof.

Cove Point Lighthouse was built in 1828.

Building the town created new jobs and gave people affordable places to live.

On December 7, 1941, the Japanese bombed the US naval base in Pearl Harbor, Hawaii. The USS *Maryland*, named after the state, was one of the battleships damaged in the attack. The next day, the United States entered World War II. During the war, some fifty-five thousand Marylanders served in the armed forces. Many more worked in shipbuilding, aircraft manufacturing, and other wartime industries. Women took over the jobs of many men who were called to fight overseas. After the war ended in 1945, the state had more jobs than people to fill them. Maryland's cities and towns grew bigger than ever. From 1940 to 1950, the state's population grew by more than five hundred thousand.

The Civil Rights Movement

Despite the state's growing prosperity after World War II, many African Americans felt left behind. Like many other states, Maryland had laws that forced blacks and whites to use separate public facilities. These included train cars, restaurants, and schools. This system of separation was called **segregation**. Under segregation, the quality of services offered to blacks was not as good as what was offered to whites. Maryland's African Americans had long been fighting to gain the same treatment as whites. The National Association for the Advancement of Colored People (NAACP) is an organization that fights for civil rights. The NAACP's second-oldest chapter had been founded in Baltimore in 1913. Baltimore is now the organization's home.

Marylander Thurgood Marshall was the first African American appointed to the Supreme Court.

NAACP attorney Thurgood Marshall, from Baltimore, was a leader in the fight for civil rights. In 1954, he won a US Supreme Court decision against segregation in public schools. In 1967, President Lyndon Johnson appointed Marshall to the US Supreme Court. He was the first African American to serve on the court. Marshall served on the Supreme Court for twenty-four years before retiring in 1991 at age eighty-three.

Though African Americans had made gains in racial equality in the 1950s, their struggle was far from over. Civil rights leader Martin Luther King Jr. was assassinated in Memphis, Tennessee, in 1968. His murder led to riots in Baltimore and other US cities. The riots had a lasting negative effect on Baltimore, which was already struggling. The city's population had

Harborplace was part of a plan to bring new life to the city of Baltimore.

peaked in the years after World War II. In 1950, Baltimore was the sixth-largest city in the United States. But as large numbers of white people moved to neighboring areas, or suburbs, the population began to fall.

As suburbs prospered, Baltimore began to suffer. Many African Americans either could not afford to move to suburbs or were not allowed to because of **discrimination**. The manufacturing jobs that had been so vital to the city's economy disappeared. The economy of the whole state suffered in the 1970s. Many businesses closed or moved to other states, leaving thousands of Marylanders out of work.

In the 1970s, the government took steps to attract businesses and tourism to Baltimore. In the mid-1970s, the city celebrated the opening of the Baltimore Convention Center and the Baltimore World Trade Center. At 400 feet (123 m), the Baltimore World Trade Center is the tallest building with five even sides (pentagon) in the world. In 1980, a new business area called Harborplace opened in what had become a run-down area of the old harbor (or Inner Harbor) in Baltimore. Tourists flocked to its shops and restaurants. The National Aquarium opened in the Inner Harbor district the following year. In the 1990s, the city built new stadiums for its baseball team, the Orioles, and its new professional football team, the Ravens. But even as tourism increased, the city's population continued to fall. In 2016, Baltimore ranked thirtieth in the nation.

Looking to the Future

Today, Maryland is home to many high-tech industries. Jobs related to computers, lab work, scientific research, and more have replaced heavy industry in its cities. The federal government has many scientific agencies that are headquartered in Maryland. The National Institutes of Health in Bethesda performs medical research. Scientists and engineers at the Goddard Space Flight Center in Greenbelt develop new instruments and technology to study Earth and outer space.

Goddard Space Flight Center in Greenbelt is part of NASA.

In May of 2017, Maryland governor Larry Hogan announced a new initiative to bring business to the state. Called "Excel Maryland," the initiative brings the state's universities, businesses, and local government together to encourage growth. Already a leader in high-tech industry, Maryland hopes to further develop its economy in cutting-edge fields. Two industries that the initiative focuses on are life sciences—like biotech—and **cybersecurity**.

Maryland's Important People

Clara Barton

Clara Barton was a nurse who rose to fame for her work during the American Civil War. She cared for Union soldiers and went on a speaking tour about her experience during the war. Later, she started the American Red Cross. The organization operated out of her Maryland home. Today, the house is a national historic site.

Clara Barton

Stephen Decatur

Stephen Decatur was born on the Eastern Shore of Maryland. He joined the US Navy at a young age and went on to have a distinguished military career. He fought in a number of conflicts—including the Barbary War in Africa and the War of 1812. Decatur has been described as one of the first national heroes after the Revolutionary War, and many cities and ships have been named in his honor.

Stephen Decatur

Frederick Douglass

Born as a slave in Maryland, Frederick Douglass went on to escape slavery and become a national icon. His published account of his life as a slave was a best-selling book. He became a prominent leader of the **abolitionist** movement against slavery and a larger-than-life figure in African American history.

Billie Holiday

Billie Holiday spent her early years in Baltimore, Maryland. She had a difficult life living in poverty, and she dropped out of school in the fifth grade. However, she overcame her difficult childhood and went on to become a famous singer. She toured the United States and Europe. After her death, she was inducted into the Grammy Hall of Fame.

Thurgood Marshall

Thurgood Marshall grew up in Baltimore, Maryland. He went on to study law and become a leading African American lawyer in the fight for civil rights. He argued the *Brown v. Board of Education of Topeka* case that banned segregation in schools before the Supreme Court. Later, he was the first African American appointed to serve on the Supreme Court.

Edgar Allan Poe

Edgar Allan Poe struggled to make a living as an author, leading him to live in a number of different cities. He spent considerable time in Baltimore, where he was later buried. Poe wrote poems and short stories that are famous for their mysterious elements. He is remembered as one of the most important American authors of his time.

Frederick Douglass

Babe Ruth

Named George Herman Ruth Jr. at birth, "Babe" Ruth would become one of the most famous figures in American sports history. He was born in Baltimore, Maryland, and played for a minor-league team there before he went on to the major leagues. He was famous for both his pitching and hitting abilities.

Harriet Tubman

Harriet Tubman was born into slavery in Maryland. After escaping around the age of twenty-seven, she helped lead other slaves to freedom. She was a conductor on the Underground Railroad, which aided escaping slaves in the South. Tubman was also active during the Civil War. She nursed Union soldiers and even led a raid to free slaves in South Carolina.

Harriet Tubman

These students at Tridelphia Ridge Elementary School are studying cursive. Education is very important in Maryland.

3 Who Lives in Maryland?

art of Maryland's strength is its diversity. All sorts of people with different backgrounds call Maryland home. Some can trace their ancestry back to early settlers who came to the New World, while others are first- or second-generation immigrants. Marylanders descend from people from all over the world, including many countries in Europe, Africa, and Asia. They often celebrate their distinctive cultures while living in diverse communities. Ethnic restaurants are a common sight across the state, and immigrant communities often hold festivals to keep their traditions alive.

Native Americans

Before the Europeans arrived, there were more than twenty Native American groups on the land that is now Maryland. Many tribes were forced to move as Europeans began to settle in the area. Today, less than 1 percent of Maryland's population is Native American.

Before the American colonies were established, the Accohannock tribe is said to have lived on the Eastern Shore of Maryland and Virginia. The tribe is currently trying to obtain state and federal recognition. Federal recognition would enable the tribe to claim a legal relationship to the US government and receive federal aid. (However, some critics say that the Accohannock tribe lived only on the Eastern Shore of Virginia. These people feel that the Accohannock tribe, therefore, should not receive state recognition.)

Every year, the Accohannock tribe holds the Native American Heritage Festival and Powwow. At this event, the Accohannocks celebrate their traditions and culture. Members of the tribe also attend powwows in other states and present their culture to schools and other organizations.

Michael Steele is a prominent politician from Maryland.

African Americans

African Americans are Maryland's largest minority. They make up over 30 percent of the population. Some African Americans have moved from Washington, DC, to nearby Prince George's County in southeastern Maryland. Once mostly white, Prince George's County is now more than 65 percent black. In Baltimore, nearly two-thirds of the residents are black.

Wayne K. Curry was the first African American to hold the Prince George's County executive position. He served from 1994 to 2002. In 2003, Michael Steele became Maryland's lieutenant governor. That is the second-highest office in the state government. Steele was the first African American to be elected to a statewide office in Maryland. He is a member of the

Many different recipes in Maryland call for blue crab meat, from crab cakes to crab bisque. One party favorite is crab dip. It is relatively easy to make, and it's a delicious appetizer for any meal.

Maryland Crab Dip

Ingredients

- 1 pound of lump or backfin crab meat
- 8 oz. cream cheese
- ½ cup mayonnaise
- 2 teaspoons Old Bay seasoning
- ½ cup cheddar cheese
- Crackers
- Mixing bowl
- 1½ quart baking dish

Directions

1. Soften the cream cheese in the microwave for about 20 seconds.
2. In a mixing bowl, combine the cream cheese with the Old Bay and mayonnaise.
3. Fold in the crab meat gently until everything is mixed together.
4. Add the mixture to a 1½ quart baking dish and spread it evenly. Top with the cheddar cheese.
5. Bake in the oven for 30 minutes at 350°F. The cheese should be bubbly on top when it is ready.
6. Serve your crab dip with any kind of cracker you like!

In the Chesapeake Bay, there is a small community of people who live on Smith Island. The island can only be reached by boat, and it was first settled in the mid-1600s. The people who live there are known for their distinctive speech. Many features can be traced back to early English settlers. But as younger residents move to the mainland, the dialect is in danger of dying out.

Republican Party—one of the two main political parties in the United States. (The other is the Democratic Party.) In 2009, Steele became the first African American to chair the Republican National **Committee**, which sets the party's platform, or goals, and raises money.

Baltimore

About nine of every ten Marylanders live in or near a city. The rest live in rural areas. Annapolis, the state capital, is small. It has only about 39,000 people. Baltimore is the state's largest city, with a population of almost 612,000.

Baltimore is known as the city of neighborhoods. Many of those neighborhoods were formed in the 1800s by European immigrants who wanted to live near people from their homelands. They wanted to be able to speak their native languages and help each other find jobs and places to live. Today, there are more than 225 neighborhoods in the city.

Many Irish people once lived in southwestern Baltimore. They helped build the Baltimore and Ohio Railroad. The houses they once lived in were supposed to be torn down. However, local residents worked to restore them. The railroad's old engine roundhouse nearby has been turned into a museum. A roundhouse is a circular building that is used for storing and repairing locomotives.

Another museum in Baltimore is dedicated to African

The Booker T. Washington exhibit at Baltimore's National Great Blacks in Wax Museum

Americans. The National Great Blacks in Wax Museum has more than one hundred life-size wax figures of famous African Americans, including many from Maryland. One of the figures is of Matthew Henson. In 1909, he was among the first explorers to reach the North Pole, as part of an expedition led by Robert Peary.

The Gallery at Harborplace

Downtown Baltimore has many things to see, such as Harborplace and Camden Yards, the home of the Orioles baseball team. The National Aquarium is seven stories high and has an Atlantic coral reef with 335,000 gallons (1.3 million liters) of water and hundreds of tropical reef fish. Visitors can also walk through a South American rain forest encased in glass or explore an Australian Outback river gorge.

The Orioles played their first game at Camden Yards in 1992.

Music lovers may enjoy the Baltimore Symphony Orchestra, which plays classical music. Fans of jazz can see live performances at the Eubie Blake National Jazz Institute and Cultural Center. Eubie Blake was a famous ragtime and jazz composer who was popular in the early twentieth century.

Dolphin Discovery is the National Aquarium's largest exhibit.

Maryland's Changing Population

Maryland's population has changed rapidly in recent years. In 1970, 96 percent of the state's population was African American or non-Hispanic white. This means just 4 percent of the state's population did not belong to one of these two groups. The state was diverse in that 22.7 percent of the state was African American. However, other minority groups were hardly represented in the state.

In 2016, the number of people who are not African American or non-Hispanic white was 17.8 percent. This is a huge increase from 4 percent just forty-six years previously. The biggest growth was among Hispanics or Latinos and people of Asian descent. In 1970, just 1.5 percent of Maryland's population was Asian, and 1.5 percent was Hispanic or Latino. In 2016, 6.6 percent of the state's population was Asian and 9.8 percent was Hispanic or Latino! The percentage of African Americans in the state also increased from 22.7 percent to 30.7 percent.

Many different things drove these changes in Maryland's population. One of the biggest was increased migration to the counties near Washington, DC. The biggest population growth in Maryland is occurring in this area. Counties like Montgomery County have seen explosive growth. People of Asian and Hispanic descent have come to the area in much larger numbers than non-Hispanic whites. This has made Montgomery County both the most populous county in the state and incredibly diverse. The county is home to more than a million people, and it has a minority majority, meaning non-Hispanic whites make up less than 50 percent of the population.

The trend in Maryland has been a sharp increase in population—especially minority groups—around Washington, DC. Meanwhile, the population of Baltimore has actually been declining over the past century. People are slowly leaving the city to move elsewhere.

The picture in rural counties across Maryland is mixed. Some counties are almost exclusively non-Hispanic white—and sparsely populated. For instance, Garrett County in the western mountains of the state has around thirty thousand people, making it just 3 percent the size of Montgomery County. Garrett County's population is over 96 percent non-Hispanic white.

On the other hand, rural counties on the Eastern Shore rather than in the western mountains tend to be diverse. Not only is there a large African American population but also growing immigrant communities. Thousands of people from Haiti and Latin American countries have come to the peninsula in recent years for jobs. The poultry industry, in particular, is responsible for drawing many immigrants to the area.

This map shows the racial diversity of Maryland's counties, as of 2016.

Black 50–60%
Black 60–70%
Non-Hispanic White 40–50%
Non-Hispanic White 50–60%
Non-Hispanic White 60–70%
Non-Hispanic White 70–80%
Non-Hispanic White 80–90%
Non-Hispanic White >90%

Excellence in Education

The US Naval Academy in Annapolis

Education is important in Maryland. One of the first US public high schools opened in Baltimore in 1839. Western High School, which opened in 1844, is the oldest all-girls public high school in the country. There are more than 1,400 public schools and more than 1,200 private schools throughout the state. Since 2003, Maryland has funded charter schools as well. Charter schools are public (tax-supported) schools run by independent groups rather than local school boards. They have specific educational goals.

In 2012, a higher percentage of Maryland high school students passed their Advanced Placement (AP) exams than in any other state. Students who pass AP exams can earn credit toward a college degree.

More than one in three adult Marylanders is a college graduate. That is one of the highest percentages in the nation. Today, college-bound students can choose from more than a dozen universities in Maryland. Since 1999, students in Maryland have been able to take college courses on the internet.

George Washington helped found the first college in the state in 1782. It is called Washington College in his honor. Mount Saint Mary's in Emmitsburg is the country's second-oldest Catholic college. The University

FAST FACT

On October 1, 2008, the Smith Island cake was named Maryland's state dessert. Most cakes have two or three layers with icing in between them. But a Smith Island cake has eight or more layers of cake—each with a matching layer of icing. The result is an exceptionally delicious cake!

Maryland's Biggest Colleges and Universities

(All enrollment numbers are from US News and World Report *2018 college rankings.)*

1. University of Maryland University College
Adelphi (44,219 undergraduate students)

University of Maryland University College

2. University of Maryland, College Park
College Park (28,472 undergraduate students)

3. Towson University
Towson (19,198 undergraduate students)

University of Maryland, College Park

4. University of Maryland, Baltimore County
Baltimore (11,142 undergraduate students)

5. Salisbury University
Salisbury (7,861 undergraduate students)

6. Morgan State University
Baltimore (6,362 undergraduate students)

7. Johns Hopkins University
Baltimore (6,117 undergraduate students)

Towson University

8. Frostburg State University
Frostburg (4,884 undergraduate students)

9. Bowie State University,
Bowie, (4,711 undergraduate students)

10. United States Naval Academy
Annapolis (4,526 undergraduate students)

Salisbury University

of Maryland University College in Prince George's County is the largest college in the state, with more than forty-four thousand undergraduate students.

The second-largest college is the University of Maryland's flagship campus, located in College Park. It was founded in 1859. The University of Maryland, Baltimore County, is one of the most diverse colleges in the country. A large percentage of its students are either Asian American or African American. Annapolis is the home of the US Naval Academy. Cadets spend their summers training on ships at sea. When they graduate, cadets become officers in the US Navy or the Marine Corps.

Sports and Recreation

Marylanders like to work and study, but they also like to play. The state is home to the Baltimore Orioles baseball team and the Baltimore Ravens football team. The Redskins football team may be from Washington, DC, but the team plays its home games in Landover, Maryland. A half-dozen Minor League Baseball teams are also based in the state, from the Hagerstown Suns to the Delmarva Shorebirds in Salisbury.

Horse racing has been a tradition at Pimlico Race Course in Baltimore since 1870. The first Preakness Stakes was held three years later. Tens of thousands of fans still crowd the stands and the track's grassy infield to watch the Preakness. It is the second race of horse racing's Triple Crown series.

Annapolis's beautiful harbor is one of the top centers for sailing on the East Coast. Visitors can sail aboard the schooner *Woodwind*, a **replica** of

Celebrities from Maryland

Julie Bowen

Born in Baltimore, Julie Bowen has made a name for herself in TV and movies. She has won two Emmy Awards for her work on TV. Bowen is also the voice of several animated characters. Recently, she was the voice of Queen Arianna in Disney's *Tangled: The Series*.

Julie Bowen

Kevin Durant

NBA star Kevin Durant was born in Suitland in 1988. While in college, Durant was drafted by the Seattle SuperSonics in 2007. The SuperSonics later relocated and became the Oklahoma City Thunder. In 2016, Durant joined the Golden State Warriors. He has played on the NBA All-Star team eight times and has been a scoring champion four times.

Kevin Durant

Anna Faris

Actress, author, and producer Anna Faris was born in Baltimore. She is best known for starring in comedies, both on television and on the big screen. Faris has also lent her voice to a number of animated characters.

Anna Faris

Michael Phelps

Michael Phelps was born in Baltimore and began to swim competitively at a young age. When he was just ten years old, he claimed a national record for a swimming event in his age group. He went on to have one of the most successful careers in the history of athletics. He won a total of twenty-eight Olympic medals—the most of anyone in history.

Mike Rowe

Maryland native Mike Rowe was a professional opera singer, but he is best known for his work on TV. Rowe hosted the shows *Dirty Jobs* and *Somebody's Gotta Do It*, among others.

Michael Phelps

The Terrapins were the 2017 NCAA Division I champions in men's lacrosse.

a luxury yacht from the early 1900s. During their tour of the harbor, amateur sailors can help the crew raise the sails and even take turns steering the ship.

One of the state's most popular sports—lacrosse—is the oldest team sport in North America. It was invented by Native Americans. Each player uses a stick with a net attached at one end to throw a ball into the opposite team's goal. Johns Hopkins University, the University of Maryland, Baltimore County, the University of Maryland, College Park, and Loyola College have some of the best men's college lacrosse teams. In 2017, the powerhouse University of Maryland Lady Terrapins won their thirteenth Division I NCAA national championship in lacrosse.

Jousting at the Maryland Renaissance Festival

Maryland's state sport is jousting. This sport was developed in the Middle Ages when knights on horseback tried to knock each other to the ground with long metal-tipped wooden spears called lances. Marylanders have enjoyed jousting since colonial times. They play a less violent form of jousting. Riders attempt to "spear" hanging rings with a lance. Each rider must do this while galloping on horseback. The one who lifts the most rings is the champion.

Future Growth

Maryland's population growth is lower than average for the United States. Between 2015 and 2016, Maryland's population grew by just 0.36 percent. This is below the national average of 0.7 percent. However, Maryland grew much more than some other states. Eight states actually declined in population during the same period. Maryland is also the fifth most densely populated state, so it is unsurprising that it is not growing quickly.

In the future, Maryland expects to see continued slow growth. Its population will become more and more diverse as time goes on. Crowded counties like Montgomery County are expected to grow more slowly than less crowded counties. The highest growth rate is expected in Southern Maryland and some rural counties of the Eastern Shore. The population of Baltimore is also expected to stabilize and gradually increase, reversing its current trend of declining population.

Johns Hopkins Hospital is
a leader in medicine.

4 At Work in Maryland

Maryland has an exceptionally strong economy. On average, households in Maryland are some of the best off in the country. In 2016, the median household income in Maryland was $73,760—the fourth highest of any state. People in Maryland work in all kinds of fields. From high-tech jobs to farming and fishing, Maryland's economy truly has it all.

Jobs in Maryland

Maryland has many doctors, mathematicians, biologists, and other scientists who do a lot of research and development. In fact, Maryland ranks first in the country in the percentage of scientists, technicians, and other professional workers. Around 8.6 percent of Maryland workers have jobs in technology. Some work at the many federal agencies headquartered in the state. They may be employed at the Agricultural Research Service in Beltsville, where they work to improve farms. Others are involved in monitoring the weather at the National Weather Service in Silver Spring. Still others work under contract for the government in one of the several

Roll-on/roll-off cargo transportation is also called RORO. Baltimore is a major RORO site.

research parks that dot the state. The research parks are like college campuses where many companies and institutions can share information on new technologies.

Other Marylanders work in shipping. Foreign goods come and go in the big Port of Baltimore. The port specializes in a kind of cargo transportation called roll-on/roll-off. It is the leading importer of trucks, including farm and construction equipment, which can be driven, or "rolled," off the ship and onto the dock. Baltimore is a good location because it is within a day's drive of the entire Midwest and its many farms.

Other Marylanders work in service industries, such as hotels, restaurants, hospitals, resorts, museums, and schools. Some of them serve tourists who spend billions of dollars a year in the state. In 2016, about forty-two million tourists spent more than $17 billion in the state.

Agriculture

Farming is big business in Maryland. Farms cover about a third of the state. Tobacco was once the most important crop in Maryland. In 1698, minister Hugh Jones of Calvert County wrote, "Tobacco is our meat, drink, clothing and monies." This is no longer true. As more Americans understand the harmful effects of smoking cigarettes, tobacco sales are falling. There are fewer than one hundred tobacco farms left, most of which are in the southern part of the state.

Flowers and shrubs grown in nurseries are leading crops in Maryland today. Corn, soybeans, and wheat are also important. Orchards in

Solar Power in Maryland

One growing industry in Maryland is solar energy. It is a source of renewable energy, or energy that will not run out in the future. Unlike oil and coal, sunlight will always be available to create electricity. As oil and coal industries increase temperatures around the globe and result in pollution, countries and states are moving more toward clean, renewable energy like solar power. In 2016, solar energy production across the United States nearly doubled in a single year.

In Maryland, a 2017 law requires that one-quarter of the state's energy come from renewable sources by 2020. This is one reason the solar energy industry is booming in Maryland. In 2016, the industry was responsible for 1,160 new jobs in the state. It is a **burgeoning** field that has the potential to employ many Marylanders.

Sidwell Friends School in Bethesda devotes roof space to solar panels.

Solar panels are installed on top of homes and in large complexes away from neighborhoods in Maryland. The ones on top of homes drive job creation in the industry. They require a team of people to install them and work on their upkeep. By comparison, large installations on the ground produce more energy and are also easier to maintain. This means they support fewer jobs.

As renewable energy increases in the future, the Maryland solar power industry is expected to grow. It is just one high-tech way the state is looking to combat global climate change and air pollution in the state.

Trees grow at a nursery in Harford County.

northern Maryland produce apples, peaches, and other fruits.

Chickens are the state's main livestock product. In 2016, Maryland chickens laid around 796 million eggs. Around 303 million chickens, however, are raised for eating. These chickens are called broilers. These broilers amounted to 1.7 billion pounds (771 million kg) of chicken meat and over $900 million in 2016. Have you ever seen chicken that is labeled "Perdue"? Many of these chickens come from the Eastern Shore of Maryland. Perdue Farms started out as a family business and is now the fourth-largest chicken processor in the United States.

Shell Fishing

Maryland shell fishers, known as watermen, harvest more than 42 million pounds (19 million kg) of shellfish, including clams and oysters, in a year. The Chesapeake Bay is famous for its blue crabs. Crab lovers claim the meat is tastier than lobster. Marylanders think so much of their favorite shellfish that in 1989 they named it the state **crustacean**. The shellfish is even featured in a favorite state slogan: "Maryland is for crabs."

Professional crabbers go out into the Chesapeake Bay. They catch the blue crabs in crab pots. The crab enters a trap in the pot and cannot get out. People who catch crabs for fun may prefer the old-fashioned long-handled dip net. They wade into the water, and when they see a crab, they dip the net to catch it.

Many crabbers also use a hand line, or bait line. This is a long string or fishing line with a weight and bait—often a chicken neck—tied to one end. Crabbers lower the line into the water until it reaches the bottom. When a crab begins to nibble on the bait, the crabber carefully pulls up the line and scoops up the crab with a net.

A chicken house on the Eastern Shore

Made in Maryland

These watermen are sorting oysters.

Manufacturing was once a core part of Maryland's economy. Today, only about one of twenty workers in Maryland has a job in manufacturing. A large number of the state's manufacturers make computers and other high-tech electronics. Other manufacturers package foods, create printing products, or develop chemicals.

Your kitchen spice rack may be filled with spices made by McCormick and Company. This spice company in Sparks, Maryland, was started in 1889 by twenty-five-year-old Willoughby McCormick in a room and cellar in Baltimore.

McCormick and Company headquarters

Defense Industry

Maryland has long played an important role in national defense. The Glenn L. Martin Company in Baltimore produced the famous B-26 bomber and other aircraft that helped the United States win World War II. After a series of mergers, the company is now part of Lockheed Martin, based in Bethesda, Maryland. Hundreds of other aerospace and defense companies have offices in Maryland.

Lockheed Martin is a major name in the defense industry.

The Skipjack

The commercial seafood industry in Maryland has always been important. Today, there are more than four thousand professional watermen in Maryland. The industry contributes more than $600 million to the state's economy each year.

This industry also led to the invention of a Maryland symbol: the skipjack. The skipjack is a special kind of sailboat that is perfectly suited to harvesting oysters. Invented in the 1890s in Maryland, they are between 25 and 50 feet long (7.6 to 15.2 m). They have one mast and two sails and are capable of maneuvering in shallow waters.

Skipjacks dredge oysters. Dredging involves dragging a net along the bottom of the bay to gather up oysters. Skipjacks were created for this purpose. In their heyday, more than a thousand skipjacks plied the waters of the bay. Laws meant to conserve the bay restricted oyster dredging to sailboats—even once engines became common on boats. Because of this, skipjacks continued to dominate the oyster business in Maryland.

However, the oyster population eventually **dwindled** in the bay. The number of skipjacks decreased with it. A law was passed allowing skipjacks to use an engine two days of the week. As a result, a push boat was added to many skipjacks. A push boat is a small vessel that houses an engine and pushes a skipjack. Push boats with their engines made skipjacks easier to manage in port and decreased the time spent sailing to oyster beds.

Despite the use of push boats, the number of skipjacks continued to decline. Today, there are fewer than forty skipjacks in Maryland. Most do not dredge oysters anymore, but some do. This makes Maryland's skipjack fleet the last remaining workboats that still use sails. In 1985, the skipjack was made the state boat of Maryland. There are still efforts underway to increase the number of working skipjacks in the bay.

An annual skipjack race is held on Deal Island.

The state's military bases are also major employers. The workforce of military and civilian personnel at Fort Meade alone is around fifty-two thousand people. The air fleet that transports the US president and other important government leaders is based at Andrews Air Force Base, Maryland, not far from Washington, DC.

Conowingo Dam

Saving the Environment

Many people in Maryland are concerned about pollution. Waste from factories and sewage systems runs into rivers and the Chesapeake Bay, killing thousands of fish. Overfishing and illegal catching of fish that are too young also hurt the fishing industry. Maryland and neighboring Virginia, Pennsylvania, and Washington, DC, formed the Chesapeake Bay Program in 1983. The goal of the Chesapeake Bay Program is to clean up local waters. (Since 2000, New York, Delaware, and West Virginia have also gotten involved in the program.)

Open space is gradually disappearing in Maryland. The state and federal governments are working to save the land left around Baltimore and near Washington, DC. They want to preserve this land for parks and other recreational areas.

One key component of efforts to clean up the bay is the Conowingo Dam. The dam in Maryland prevents sediment from upstream from reaching the bay. However, in 2017 scientists discovered that the dam was nearly overflowing with sediment. The dam will soon stop playing its important function in protecting the bay. This is a significant blow to efforts to save the bay. It remains to be seen how Maryland and the other states of the Chesapeake Bay Program will respond to this challenge.

FAST FACT
Despite its small size, Maryland ranks fourth in the number of federal government jobs. Those are jobs that come from the federal government in Washington, DC, not the state government in Annapolis. These jobs are a key part of Maryland's economy. The high number of these jobs in Maryland is due in part to its location next to DC.

The Maryland State House in Annapolis was completed in 1779.

5 Government

Maryland's state government makes laws about many aspects of life for Marylanders. From how many fish you can catch to the penalty for breaking many laws, it is the state government that decides a lot. So long as these laws do not go against federal law, the state is largely free to do as it pleases.

Maryland counties and cities also make their own codes that people must follow. These in turn must comply with state and federal law. Unlike many states that rely largely on cities to make local laws, it is the counties in Maryland that usually serve as the local form of government. While some cities like Baltimore do have a city government, many of the largest cities in the state, like Columbia, do not have a city government at all.

FAST FACT

Maryland is one of the most Democratic-leaning states in the country. There have been six Democratic and three Republic governors in the past fifty years. The state house and senate have had a Democratic majority for more than ninety years. However, some local governments tend to lean Republican in rural areas.

County Government

Baltimore City Hall

Maryland is divided into twenty-three counties. In each county, one city or town is the county seat. Elected officials meet there to make county laws. City councils or county commissioners enforce the laws. The county government runs some towns and cities that are unincorporated. An unincorporated community does not have its own government. It does not have its own police department and other services and must rely on the county to provide them. Maryland's many unincorporated cities include Columbia, Ellicott City, Waldorf, Silver Spring, Germantown, and Glen Burnie. Towns and cities that are incorporated are run by their own governments.

Baltimore, Maryland's largest city, is not part of a county. It is an independent **municipality** run by a mayor and a city council. That is unusual, except in Virginia. Outside of Virginia, the United States has only three independent cities: Baltimore; Saint Louis, Missouri; and Carson City, Nevada.

The Maryland state legislature recognized the achievements of Olympian Michael Phelps in 2008.

State Government

The state government has a similar structure to that of the federal (national) government. Both are divided into an executive branch, a legislative branch, and a judicial branch. The Maryland state constitution functions much like the US Constitution. It describes the structure and rules of the state government. The state constitution that Maryland uses today has been in place since 1867.

The Executive Branch

The governor is the head of the executive branch. He or she carries out laws and appoints people to high office. The governor is elected to a four-year term. He or she can serve only two terms in a row.

The Legislative Branch

This branch makes the state's laws. The state legislature is called the Maryland General Assembly. It is divided into two parts. The senate has 47 members, and the house of delegates has 141 members. All general assembly members are elected to four-year terms. There is no limit on the number of terms they can serve.

The Judicial Branch

The judicial branch interprets and enforces the laws. When a person is accused of breaking a law, he or she goes on trial in one of twelve district or eight circuit courts. If someone is found guilty, the case can be appealed before the court of special appeals. If he or she is found guilty again, the person can take the case to the court of appeals. This is the highest court in the state, with seven judges.

Talbot County Courthouse

Maryland's Capital

Annapolis has been Maryland's capital since 1694. "In a few years it will probably be one of the best built cities in America," one English visitor wrote in 1769. Annapolis is one of the oldest state capitals. The governor lives there, and the general assembly meets in the Maryland State House for a period of ninety days each year, beginning in January. The Maryland State House is the oldest continuously used state house in the nation.

Annapolis was the nation's capital for a short time—from November 1783 to August 1784. During that time, Congress met in the city. On December 23, 1783, George Washington resigned as commander-in-chief of the Continental Army in Annapolis. Soon after, Congress approved the Treaty of Paris, which officially ended the Revolutionary War. The nation's capital was next moved to Trenton, New Jersey. Later it moved to New York City and then Philadelphia. In 1789, Maryland and Virginia gave land for a permanent capital city: Washington, DC.

Federal Representation

Like residents of all states, the people of Maryland are represented in the US Congress in Washington, DC. Each state elects two US senators, who serve six-year terms. There is no limit on the number of terms a US senator can serve.

A state's population determines the number of people that it sends to the US House of Representatives. As of 2018, Maryland has eight representatives in the House. They each serve two-year terms and can be elected as many times as voters choose.

Getting Involved

It is important to make your voice heard. Your representatives can only speak on your behalf if they know your views. This is why citizens contact their representatives and make their opinion known about issues that are close to their heart.

There are many different ways to contact your representative. People used to have to write a letter or pick up the phone. But now you can use a convenient website to send a message to your state representatives. The Maryland General Assembly has a website with the following address: http://www.mgaleg.maryland.gov. If you click on the tab "Legislators," you are taken to a page that has a button "Who represents me?" in the top-right corner. Once you click on this button and enter your address, you are given a list of your elected representatives.

It tells you your federal representatives—the people who represent you in Washington, DC—as well as your state representatives. The website is set up so that you can send a message to your representatives in the Maryland General Assembly. Like any other website, you should ask a trusted adult before sending a message over the internet.

Even if your representatives disagree with your opinion on an issue, it is important that they hear your view. They represent all their constituents—even the ones that have a different opinion from their own. There is a chance that if most of the messages they receive support one side, they might change their own opinion on an issue.

Marylanders gather to protest the name and mascot of the Washington Redskins.

Nonprofit Groups

Lawmakers are not the only people who have a say in Maryland's government. Ordinary citizens can do more than suggest ideas to their representatives and vote in elections. They can form citizens' groups and other organizations that promote change. Many people in Maryland are worried about the future. They see the state getting more and more crowded. New homes and business developments are taking up remaining open space. That space could be used for parks and other recreational areas.

In 1994, people who were concerned about Maryland's future got together. They did not want their state to lose all its open land to homes and businesses, so they formed a group called 1000 Friends of Maryland. The group includes businesspeople and environmental advocates. Like many activist groups, 1000 Friends of Maryland wants to make the state a better place. They want the government to fix up existing neighborhoods instead of tearing them down. They want to see the government carefully plan new communities without destroying the small amount of open space left in the state.

Another group, the Chesapeake Bay Foundation, fights to make the bay as clean and healthy as it was centuries ago. The group monitors the bay and shares what it learns with businesses, the public, and the government. The group also fights for tougher laws to protect and restore the bay.

Creating New Laws

Laws often start out as the ideas from a state's residents. When people think of new laws, they can contact their representatives in the Maryland General Assembly. The representatives then

Governor Larry Hogan

write up a proposal called a bill. A bill can start in either the senate or the house of delegates. If a bill is introduced in the house of delegates, it is read before the whole house. The bill is then presented to the leader of the house of delegates, who assigns the bill to a committee. It is the committee's responsibility to hold a hearing to discuss the bill. The committee may amend, or change, the bill. The committee may reject the bill and decide not to present it to the entire house. If the committee members approve the bill, it is sent back to the house. All members of the house of delegates vote on the bill.

If more than half the house members approve the bill, it goes to the state senate. There, it is discussed, debated, and voted on again. If the senate approves the bill, it is then presented to the governor. He or she may sign the bill or veto, or reject, it. If the governor signs it, the bill officially becomes a state law. Even if the governor vetoes the bill, it still has a chance to become a law. The rejected bill goes back to the house and senate for a new vote. If three-fifths of both the house and senate vote to overturn the veto, the bill becomes a law.

When the same party controls the legislature and the governor's mansion, vetoes tend to be uncommon. However, when the governor and the legislature are at odds, vetoes become a common occurrence. In 2015, Larry Hogan was elected governor of Maryland. Governor Hogan is a Republican, while the vast majority of the Maryland General Assembly is Democratic. The result has been a number of vetoes—even though the legislature often overturns Governor Hogan's vetoes.

One recent example of a vetoed bill was a 2017 effort to prevent Maryland colleges from asking about applicants' criminal records. Supporters of the bill hoped it would allow people who have committed crimes to further their education and get their life back on track. On May 26, 2017, Governor Hogan vetoed the bill. However, his veto was overturned by the Democratic majority in the Maryland General Assembly.

Overall, lawmakers in Maryland try to do what they think is best for everyone in the state. The government of Maryland shows how people come together to move the state forward. Maryland's future is a bright one.

Glossary

abolitionist Someone who supported the abolition, or ending, of slavery.

bombard To attack with bombs or cannons.

burgeoning Developing quickly.

committee A group of people meant to carry out a specific function.

crustacean A member of the family of animals that includes lobsters, crabs, shrimp, and barnacles.

cybersecurity An industry that protects computers and networks from hacking and theft.

Delmarva Peninsula A region made up of parts of Delaware, Maryland, and Virginia that stretches more than 180 miles (290 km) in length and 70 miles (113 km) in width.

discrimination The unfair treatment of someone due to a personal characteristic like his or her race or gender.

dwindled Shrank.

municipality A city or town with a local government.

replica A copy of something.

segregation The separation of people based on their race. In the United States, businesses and even the government used to segregate blacks and whites.

tuberculosis A disease that usually affects the lungs. It is no longer common in the United States.

Underground Railroad A network of secret routes and people who helped slaves travel from one "station," or safe hiding place, to another on their way to freedom in the North.

unincorporated A town or city that is unincorporated has no local city government. Instead, it is governed by the county.

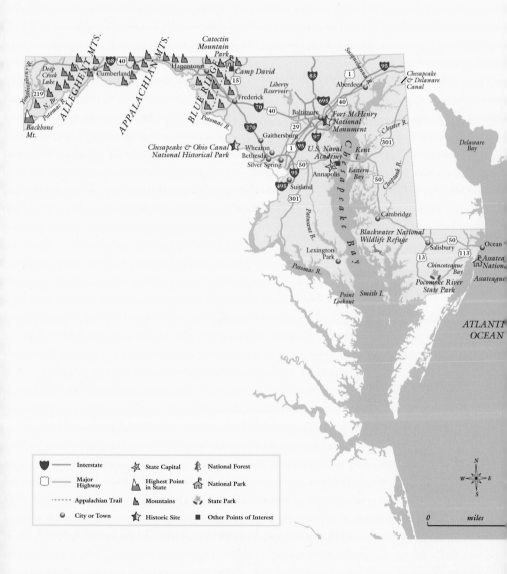

Catoctin
Mountain
Park

Camp David

*Liberty
Reservoir*

ALLEGHENY MTS.

APPALACHIAN MTS.

BLUE RIDGE

Youghiogheny R.

*Deep
Creek
Lake*

219

N. Br.
Potomac R.

*Backbone
Mt.*

68 40
Cumberland

Hagerstown

15

Frederick

70 40

270
Gaithersburg

*Chesapeake & Ohio Canal
National Historical Park*

Wheaton
Bethesda

Silver Spring

1 95

50

95

495 Suitland

301

Potomac R.

Susquehanna R.

83

1

95

*Chesapeake
& Delaware
Canal*

Aberdeen

695 40

Baltimore

29

*Fort McHenry
National
Monument*

*U.S. Naval
Academy*

Annapolis

*Kent
I.*

Chester R.

301

*Eastern
Bay*

50

Choptank R.

*Delaware
Bay*

97

Chesapeake Bay

Cambridge

*Blackwater National
Wildlife Refuge*

Lexington
Park

Patuxent R.

Potomac R.

*Point
Lookout*

Smith I.

Salisbury 50

13

*Chincoteague
Bay*

113

Ocean

Assatea
Nationa

*Pocomoke River
State Park*

Assateague

*ATLANTI
OCEAN*

	Interstate		State Capital		National Forest
	Major Highway		Highest Point in State		National Park
	Appalachian Trail		Mountains		State Park
	City or Town		Historic Site		Other Points of Interest

N
W   E
S

0   *miles*

Maryland State Map and Map Skills

Map Skills

1. What national park is to the south of Ocean City?

2. Which mountain range is to the east of the Appalachian Mountains?

3. To get from Salisbury to Cambridge, which highway would you take?

4. What is Maryland's highest point?

5. To get to Bethesda from the state capital, what direction would you travel?

6. On this map, what historic site is closest to Baltimore?

7. The Susquehanna River flows into what bay?

8. What direction is Cambridge from the Blackwater National Wildlife Refuge?

9. The Chesapeake & Ohio Canal National Historical Park is along what river?

10. What is the southernmost city or town labeled on the map?

Answers

1. Assateague Island National Seashore
2. Blue Ridge Mountains
3. Highway 50
4. Backbone Mountain
5. West
6. Fort McHenry National Monument
7. Chesapeake Bay
8. North
9. Potomac River
10. Lexington Park

Further Information

Books

Doak, Robin S. *Exploring the Maryland Colony*. Mankato, MN: Capstone Press, 2016.

Heinrichs, Ann, and Matt Kania. *USA Travel Guides: Maryland*. North Mankato, MN: The Child's World, 2017.

Marsico, Katie. *The Chesapeake Bay*. Ann Arbor, MI: Cherry Lake Publishing, 2013.

Websites

The Colonial Kids' Guide to St. Mary's City
http://www.hsmcdigshistory.org/programs-tours/tours/student-resources/kids-guide
Learn about life in historic Saint Mary's City, the first city in Maryland.

The Secretary of State: Kids Pages
http://sos.maryland.gov/mdkids
Maryland's secretary of state provides a website for kids with information and activities about Maryland.

Statewide Park Events and Programs
http://dnr.maryland.gov/publiclands/Pages/outdooreduc.aspx
Discover educational activities available in Maryland's state parks.

Things to Do: Family Fun
http://www.visitmaryland.org/things-to-do/family-fun
Maryland's Department of Tourism website outlines some fun trips and activities in the state.

Index

Page numbers in **boldface** are illustrations. Entries in **boldface** are glossary terms.